© Copyright 2025 - All rights reserved.

The content contained within this book may not be reproduced, duplicated, or transmitted without direct written permission from the author or the publisher.

Under no circumstances will any blame or legal responsibility be held against the publisher, or author, for any damages, reparation, or monetary loss due to the information contained within this book, either directly or indirectly.

Legal Notice:

This book is copyright protected. It is only for personal use. You cannot amend, distribute, sell, use, quote, or paraphrase any part, or the content within this book, without the consent of the author or publisher.

Disclaimer Notice:

Please note the information contained within this document is for educational and entertainment purposes only. All effort has been executed to present accurate, up-to-date, reliable, and complete information. No warranties of any kind are declared or implied. Readers acknowledge that the author is not engaging in the rendering of legal, financial, medical, or professional advice. The content within this book has been derived from various sources. Please consult a licensed professional before attempting any techniques outlined in this book.

By reading this document, the reader agrees that under no circumstances is the author responsible for any losses, direct or indirect, that are incurred as a result of the use of the information contained within this document, including, but not limited to, errors, omissions, or inaccuracies.

Table of Contents

Introduction — 1

Chapter 1: Mexico Before the Aztecs — 2

Chapter 2: The Mexica in the Valley of Mexico — 11

Chapter 3: The Founding of Tenochtitlán — 19

Chapter 4: The Expansion of the Aztecs — 26

Chapter 5: Aztec Arts, Crafts, and Trade — 35

Chapter 6: Aztec Society and Political Organization — 43

Chapter 7: Aztec Religion and Deities — 51

Chapter 8: A Day in the Life of the Aztecs — 60

Chapter 9: The Spanish Conquest — 67

Chapter 10: Legacy of the Aztec Empire — 76

If you want to learn more about tons of other exciting historical periods, check out our other books! — 83

Bibliography — 84

Image Sources — 86

INTRODUCTION

Welcome to the exciting world of the Aztecs! This book, Aztecs for Kids, is your ticket to a fun-filled journey back in time. This content is designed especially for young readers, learners, and explorers just like you! It has plenty of fun activities, stunning pictures, and interesting facts that will make learning about Aztec history an awesome adventure.

Imagine yourself as a time-traveling adventurer. Witnessing the major events that happened in the majestic Aztec world and shaped their complex civilization! This book breathes life into Aztec history by making it easy to understand and engaging. You'll find captivating images, detailed maps, and up-to-date information that will educate and entertain you.

But that's not all! Aztecs for Kids is more than just a book. It's an interactive learning adventure. With cool activities that challenge your creativity and thinking, you'll be having so much fun that you won't even realize you're learning!

So, are you ready to embark on this adventure? Remember, reading and learning about history helps you to understand the world you live in today. Let's dive in and explore the extraordinary world of the Aztecs.

Enjoy your Aztec adventure!

Chapter 1: Early Egypt and the Old Kingdom

The Aztecs thrived in Mesoamerica in the 15th century. The areas from central Mexico up to present-day Central America are collectively referred to as Mesoamerica. Several diverse and complex societies lived in Mesoamerica. They shaped the culture and history of the region over thousands of years.

Before the *Aztecs (as-tek-s)*, Mexico was inhabited by many diverse nations. They laid remarkable cultural and historical foundations, which the Aztecs built upon and refined. Even though these great civilizations lived a long time ago, aspects of their societies can be seen in the societies that came after them.

Ancient pyramid ruins dating back to the Toltec period in Mesoamerica.[1]

Let's look at some of the pre-Aztec civilizations and the influence they had on the powerful Aztecs!

The Olmec Civilization

The *Olmec (ohl-mek)* were a tribe of people who traveled from northern Mexico and eventually settled in the Gulf of Mexico. They are believed to date back as far as 1600 BCE! They were a thriving civilization between 1200 and 400 BCE.

Their home in the humid lowlands was full of lush tropical forests. This area is what we refer to as the Mexican states of Veracruz and Tabasco. They grew crops, such as beans, maize (corn), and squash.

Fun Fact

" The Olmecs manufactured rubber from latex extracted from an indigenous (naturally occurring in the region) rubber tree called Castilla elastica (kas-tee-ya eh-las-tee-ka). "

An Olmec colossal head. This one is almost six feet tall![2]

The Olmecs constructed large cities and built a complex society. They are well known for the artwork they produced. They carved massive stone heads with human features that weigh between six and forty tons each! They also used a green stone called jade to produce beautiful ornaments and figurines.

The Olmec civilization knew how to have fun. They are believed to have been the first major Mesoamerican civilization to play an ancient ball game. This ball game was later played by the Aztecs and other societies in Mesoamerica. The Olmecs used a ten-pound solid rubber ball and had between one and four people on each team.

Fun Fact

> The word "Olmec" is a word in the Nahuatl (nah-wa-tul) language. The word means "rubber people" in English. The Nahuatl language was spoken by several tribes in Mexico. We will learn more about the Nahuatl language and get to know more Nahuatl words throughout the rest of this book!

The Olmecs built some of the first large pyramid structures. These served as ceremonial places to gather and worship the gods. The Aztecs added their own touches to the Olmec pyramid design.

The Olmecs developed and used a 365-day earthly calendar and a separate religious calendar that *demarcated* (outlined) rituals to be performed over a 260-day cycle. The Aztecs and other Mesoamerican civilizations used both of these calendar systems too.

The Toltec Civilization

The *Toltec (tohl-tek)* society was regarded by the Aztecs as their forefathers! They flourished between the 10th and 12th centuries in central Mexico just outside the present-day Mexican city of Tula. They established their capital city, which they proudly named *Tula (too-luh)*. It is also referred to as *Tollan (tohl-lahn)*. This capital city was dazzling and full of life.

Statues of Toltec warriors. [3]

The Toltecs were great warriors, skilled builders, and expert craftsmen. They created artwork and assembled smaller creations using metal. They built serpent columns and large statues.

Fun Fact
"The word "Toltec" is a word in the Nahuatl language. It means "a person from Tula" in English."

The Aztecs revered the Toltec civilization so much that they also worshiped the Toltec god known as the "Feathered Serpent." This god was called *Quetzalcoatl (kwet-sahl-koh-ah-tul)*. You will read more about him in Chapter 7.

The Aztecs also used the Toltecs' agricultural methods, including their irrigation systems and their soil conservation practice of hill terracing.

The Maya Civilization

The *Maya (mai-uh)* society thrived in the southeast of Mexico and other parts of Mesoamerica from around 250 to 900 CE. They are known for their superior grasp of astronomy and mathematics. Their precise methods of timekeeping and calendars show just how sophisticated they were. They also built large temples and pyramids. Their writing was highly developed too.

Millions of Maya descendants inhabit Mexico and Central America today. The Maya set a high bar for developments in areas like science and culture in Mesoamerica. The Aztecs were influenced by many Maya practices. They were influenced by their *hieroglyphs* (using pictures and symbols instead of letters and words) and architectural styles.

The Teotihuacanos

The ancient nation of *Teotihuacanos (te-aw-tee-wah-kahn-os)* lived just northeast of what we refer to today as Mexico City. They were a dominant society in the city of *Teotihuacan (te-aw-tee-wah-kahn)* from about 400 BCE to 750 CE in modern Mexico. It is still not known who built this city or who lived there before the Aztecs found the ruins. The Aztecs labeled the city and its inhabitants, and we continue to use those names to this day!

Fun Fact

> Both names are words in the Nahuatl language. The word "Teotihuacan" means "birthplace of the gods" in English. The word "Teotihuacanos" is a derivation (the formation of a new word from an existing word) of the city's name. It refers to the population of the society that founded and lived in this city.

Excavations revealed that the city of Teotihuacan was a metropolis over twice the size of Disneyland! It had a population of up to 200,000 inhabitants. The city had plazas, temples, palaces, markets, and large residential complexes. The city was designed in an intricate grid with a large road leading to an extinct volcano.

Teotihuacan City (aerial view).[4]

The Teotihuacanos were exceptionally good at architecture. They erected colossal pyramids that were like skyscrapers. These pyramids towered over everything else in the city. Two of the most significant pyramids they built were named the Pyramid of the Moon and the Pyramid of the Sun.

The Aztecs truly respected the Teotihuacanos. When they found the ruins of Teotihuacan, its design and construction left them in awe! The Aztecs believed this ancient location marked the place where time began. They viewed the site as the place where the gods had given their lives to create the sun. The Aztecs also adopted the Teotihuacanos' stepped pyramids.

The legacies of the Olmec, Toltec, Maya, and Teotihuacanos civilizations still echo throughout the heart of Mexico today. The innovative and creative contributions of these ancient civilizations have given us some insight into the history of the *Mexica (meh-shee-ka)* people, who evolved into the Aztec civilization.

Chapter 1 Activity

Mark whether the statement is true or false.

Statements	True/ False
1. The Aztec civilization existed in Mexico three thousand years ago.	
2. The Toltec society thrived during the 15th century.	
3. The Olmec civilization was an advanced society in central Mexico.	
4. Central Mexico falls within the region known as Mesoamerica.	
5. The history of Mexico spans about 1,500 years.	
6. The Toltec capital city was known as Toltec City.	
7. The Olmecs made and used rubber.	
8. The word "Teotihuacan" means "the moon and stars" in English.	
9. The Toltec civilization did not believe in religion or gods.	
10. The Aztec Empire thrived in the 15th century.	

Chapter 1 Answers

Statements	True/ False
1. The Aztec civilization existed in Mexico three thousand years ago.	False
2. The Toltec society thrived during the 15th century.	False
3. The Olmec civilization was an advanced society in central Mexico.	True
4. Central Mexico falls within the region known as Mesoamerica.	True
5. The history of Mexico spans about 1,500 years.	False
6. The Toltec capital city was known as Toltec City.	False
7. The Olmecs made and used rubber.	True
8. The word "Teotihuacan" means "the moon and stars" in English.	False
9. The Toltec civilization did not believe in religion or gods.	False
10. The Aztec Empire thrived in the 15th century.	True

Chapter 2: The Mexica in the Valley of Mexico

Beginning around the early 12th century CE, several people from parts situated north of central Mexico started exploring. They wanted to find a new place to settle and call home. They were originally known as the *Chichimecas (chee-chee-mekas)* in their homeland. A large portion of these people ultimately came together in the Valley of Mexico. They chose this area to build their community. They collectively became known as the *Mexica (meh-shee-ka)* people.

The Mexica and the Aztecs

The words "Mexica" and "Aztecs" are often used interchangeably. It was only in the 1800s that a man named Albert von Humboldt created the name "Aztecs." So, up until the 19th century, only the word "Mexica" was used. It is accurate to regard the Mexica as a part of the Aztec civilization.

Today, it is acknowledged that the Aztec civilization includes the Mexica, who founded the great city of *Tenochtitlán (te-nawch-tee-tlahn)*. We will discover more about this sophisticated city in the next chapter.

The Mexica (the Aztecs) are part of a larger population group known as the Nahua.

> **Fun Fact**
>
> The Valley of Mexico is the same as the Basin of Mexico. Both terms refer to the same geographic region in modern Mexico.

The Nahua Population

The *Nahua (nah-u-wa)* people are a large and ancient group in Mexico. They relocated from the north of central Mexico around the beginning of the 6th century.

The Nahua were originally known as the Chichimecas in their homeland. That's right; just like the Mexica (Aztecs)!

The Nahua called their homeland *Aztlan (ast-lan)*. It is a word in their native language, *Nahuatl (nah-wa-tul)*. It means "the place of the heron" or "the place of whiteness." It is not certain whether Aztlan existed since no discovery of such a place has been made. However, legend has it that Aztlan was a paradise. It was an island situated in a large, beautiful lake.

The Mexica, the Aztecs, and the Nahua Are All Linked!

The Nahua population includes the Mexica and the Aztecs. To understand the connection between the three, let's use an easy explanation.

Imagine the Nahua is a large circle of people. Within this circle, there is a smaller circle of people known as the Aztecs. Within this circle of Aztec people is a smaller circle of people representing the Mexica population. The people in each circle *emanate (stem)* from the larger circle of people.

In a nutshell: All Mexica are Aztecs, but not all Aztecs are Mexica. All Aztecs and all Mexica are Nahua. But not all Nahua are Aztecs or Mexica.

They have the following in common:
- They all originated in a legendary land called Aztlan, located to the north of central Mexico.
- They all spoke the Nahuatl language.

All the Nahua people in Mesoamerica speak different dialects of the Nahuatl language. This is a shared cultural characteristic of the people in Mesoamerica.

Map of the Gulf of Mexico as it was in 1519. [5]

The Nahua and then the Mexica journeyed from Aztlan and started putting down roots throughout the Basin of Mexico. The Mexica were the last significant group of migrants to settle in the Valley of Mexico. They discovered different complex tribes already inhabiting the area. These advanced tribes spoke different languages. The Mexica did not rival these tribes or take over the area. They joined the existing communities and lived amongst them. They learned a variety of new things from them.

The Mexica adopted several aspects of day-to-day life from the different tribes already living in central Mexico. Some examples of what the Mexica learned include how to farm and grow crops, such as beans, chili, and corn. They learned how to construct cities, which they built in four sections around a central square. Since they came from a roaming lifestyle, they learned what city living was all about!

Pyramid at Teopanzolco (ceremonial center of the Mexica/Aztecs).[6]

The First Mexica Rulers

The Mexica must have had leaders before they settled in the Valley of Mexico. However, clear details of who they were and how they were led have not yet come to light.

After the Mexica settled in the Basin of Mexico, they had many important and distinguished leaders. They called their male rulers *tlatoani (tla-to-aa-ne)*. The Nahuatl word means "speaker" in English. But the Mexica used the word to mean more what we would refer to in English as "king." The emperor who ruled over the Aztec Empire and was superior to the tlatoani was called *huey (hoo-ee-y)* tlatoani ("great speaker"). We will learn more about this in Chapter 6.

> **Fun Fact**
> "The earliest known ruler was a man named Tenoch (teh-nach), but it is unclear whether this ruler existed. He might have only been a mythical figure."

> **Fun Fact**
> "A man named Bernardino de Sahagún researched and wrote about the Mexica/Aztecs. He combined pictures and text into a codex (a kind of book). This book is known as the Florentine Codex. It was produced in the 16th century."

The first huey tlatoani of the Mexica (Aztecs) was called *Acamapichtli (ah-kah-mah-peech-tlee)*. The precise period during which he ruled is not certain. He was the first emperor of the Mexica (Aztecs) in their capital city, Tenochtitlán *(te-nawch-tee-tlahn)*.

Acamapichtli's governing approach was very successful. He negotiated partnerships with other groups and tribes in the region. Rather than destroy other nations, he integrated their people into his society. He increased agricultural development and expanded the city's authority. It is not certain when he died. He is thought to have died around the end of the 14th century.

His son *Huitzilihuitl (hwee-tsil-i-hwee-tul)* took the throne next. He was only sixteen years old when his dad died. He continued Tenochtitlán's growth by adopting his father's method of creating alliances with other tribes.

Huitzilihuitl died in about 1417 during a war. His son, *Chimalpopoca (ch-iy-maa-l-pow-pow-kaa)*, became the next king. He only ruled for a short period. It is widely accepted that his direct successor was a ruler named *Itzcoatl (iy-tsk-wey-tul)*. He was an important Aztec leader. In fact, he is regarded as the founder of the Aztec Empire! We will discover more about him in Chapter 4.

The Mexica integrated with and learned extensively from the tribes in the Valley of Mexico. They would continue to spread throughout central Mexico and ultimately dominate the whole area.

In the next chapter, we will uncover the amazing details of how the Mexica (Aztecs) built a colossal city at the center of the Aztec Empire.

Chapter 2 Activity

Please match the words or phrases in column A to the correct phrases in column B to complete each sentence. Insert the correct letter from column B in the spaces provided below the table.

	Column A	Column B
1.	Nahuatl	a. ...is called the huey tlatoani.
2.	Huitzilihuitl was	b. ...form part of the Nahua population.
3.	The Valley of Mexico	c. ...was Itzcoatl.
4.	In Nahuatl, the Aztec emperor	d. ...the son of the first huey tlatoani.
5.	The Mexica homeland	e. ...is the language used by the Mexica.
6.	The Mexica and the Aztecs	f. ...is part of Mesoamerica.
7.	The first Aztec emperor	g. ...speaker and refers to the king.
8.	Tlatoani means	h. ...the city of Tenochtitlán.
9.	Central Mexico	i. ...is also called the Basin of Mexico.
10.	The Mexica founded	j. ...is called Aztlan.

Chapter 2 Answers

Column A	Column B
1. Nahuatl	e. ...is the language used by the Mexica.
2. Huitzilihuitl was	d. ...the son of the first Huey Tlatoani
3. The Valley of Mexico	i. ...is also called the Basin of Mexico.
4. In Nahuatl, the Aztec emperor	a. ...is called the Huey Tlatoani.
5. The Mexica homeland	j. ...is called Aztlan.
6. The Mexica and the Aztecs	b. ...form part of the Nahua population.
7. The first Aztec emperor	c. ...was Itzcoatl.
8. Tlatoani means	g. ...speaker and refers to the king.
9. Central Mexico	f. ...is part of Mesoamerica.
10. The Mexica founded	h. ...the city of Tenochtitlán.

Chapter 3: The Founding of Tenochtitlán

The Mexica were convinced they had to find the ideal place to build their new kingdom. They believed they had to leave their native land of Aztlan and travel under the direction of their sun and war god, Huitzilopochtli.

The Legendary Founding of Tenochtitlán

Before the Mexica inhabited the Basin of Mexico, they waited for a sign from *Huitzilopochtli (wee-tsee-loh-pohch-tlee)*. The sign they were waiting for would show them where to build and expand their new empire. Not just any sign would do! Legend has it that Huitzilopochtli said they were to look for an eagle sitting on a prickly pear cactus and eating a snake.

The Mexica saw this exact scene play out on an island on Lake Texcoco's western side! And so, they decided to build their capital city, *Tenochtitlán (te-nawch-tee-tlahn)*, on this island. The Mexican coat of arms proudly incorporates the legend of Tenochtitlán's founding.

Photograph of statues depicting the founding of Tenochtitlán. [7]

> **FUN FACT**
>
> " In ancient times, Lake Texcoco was one of five natural lakes in the Basin of Mexico. The lake was gradually drained in the 17th century. Today, it is an empty basin. Most of its surface is taken up by modern Mexico City. "

Tenochtitlán was no ordinary city! It showed the inventiveness and resilience of the Mexica (Aztecs). The city was a marvel of *urban* (city) planning and engineering. The Aztecs had to drain the swampy land before they could start to construct the city. It was a hard task, but they did it!

Layout of Tenochtitlán

The city was symmetrically designed. It was divided into four *quadrants* (sections). Each of the quadrants made up a district. The four districts were separated by waterways or causeways. The districts were like the neighborhoods we have in our towns today.

The city's *epicenter* (central area) was a large square. This area was used as a ceremonial and political center. This massive courtyard area was encircled by royal palaces, temples, and houses. The city had three primary streets that connected the island city to the mainland by a causeway.

> **FUN FACT**
>
> " The Mexica/Aztecs built Tenochtitlán by hand! Construction started around 1325 CE. The construction of the city was ongoing throughout the development and expansion of the Aztec Empire. "

To create additional space for the city to expand, the Aztecs built manmade islands called *chinampas (chee-num-pa-s)*. They are often referred to as "floating gardens" because of their likeness to gardens. The chinampas were different sizes, but most were shaped like rectangles. They played a vital role in the economic expansion of Tenochtitlán and the Aztec Empire. The land was mostly used for agricultural development and production.

Painting of Tenochtitlán.[8]

Tenochtitlán was a busy city. There were several bustling markets. The Aztecs traded a variety of items at these markets. Food, clothing, pottery, sculptures, ornaments, jewelry, and even medicine were traded at these markets in exchange for other goods. The Aztecs traveled far and wide to trade for luxury items, such as gold, which they would sell or use to craft items to sell at the markets. We take a closer look at trade in the Aztec Empire in Chapter 5. Stay tuned!

The city center housed a single complex called the Templo Mayor. The Templo Mayor building projects started around 1325. The building was erected to serve as the capital city's main temple of worship. It was rebuilt several times. The original layout was always retained. It had two main temples for religious worship. It was an important place of worship for the Aztecs. Because religion was extremely important to the Aztecs, several other temples were erected throughout the city.

Another treasured site within the city was called the House of the Eagles. It was built in Tenochtitlán's holy district. This site was of huge cultural and religious significance to the Aztecs. It was a sacred meeting place for the Aztec Eagle Warriors, an exclusive group of soldiers. It consisted of life-sized terracotta sculptures of the Eagle Warriors and the Aztec god of the underworld, *Mictlantecutli (meek-tlan-tay-coo-tlee)*. The sculptures were crafted to look as lifelike as possible! The Aztecs even added shaped stucco pieces over the terracotta to *emulate* (match) the feathers on eagles' bodies.

The Aztecs built huge palaces for their leaders. The Palace of Montezuma II was a masterpiece. It had about three hundred rooms! The palace was built as the residence of the Aztec emperor who reigned from roughly 1502 until he died in 1520 CE. Read more about him in Chapter 9!

At its peak, Tenochtitlán extended over two islands in Lake Texcoco. It was larger than 130 square feet! As the city grew, so did its population. Historians estimate that the city likely had around 200,000 to 300,000 inhabitants.

Model of Tlatelolco (the main market in Tenochtitlán). ⁹

The founding of Tenochtitlán marked a major moment in the Aztec civilization's story. The city's strategic location and innovative layout showed everybody how advanced the Aztecs were.

The Aztecs did not stop at building a magnificent city! In the next chapter, we will unravel the gripping details of how the Aztecs changed from being helpers in the region to becoming the commanders of an empire.

Chapter 3 Activity

Insert the correct answer in the blank spaces provided.

1. The Mexica believed their god _____ would show them where to build their new city.

   a. Huitzilopochtli,   b. Olmec,   c. Tenochtitlán.

2. The Mexica built their new city on an island in _____.

   a. Lake Mexico,   b. Lake Aztec,   c. Lake Texcoco.

3. The Aztecs traded goods like _____.

   a. gold,   b. food,   c. jewelry.

4. The Templo Mayor consisted of _____ main temples.

   a. four,   b. six,   c. two.

5. The city of Tenochtitlán was built around a large _____.

   a. circle,   b. oval,   c. square.

6. The Aztecs named their capital city _____.

   a. Aztlan,   b. Mexico,   c. Tenochtitlán.

7. Tenochtitlán had _____ fifty thousand residents.

   a. only,   b. more than,   c. less than.

8. The Mexica are often referred to as the _____.

   a. Aztecs,   b. Toltecs,   c. Olmecs.

9. The Aztec god of the underworld is _____.

   a. Tlatoani,   b. Huitzilopochtli,   c. Mictlantecutli.

Chapter 3 Answers

1. The Mexica believed their god **Huitzilopochtli** would show them where to build their new city.

   a. Huitzilopochtli

2. The Mexica built their new city on an island in **Lake Texcoco**.

   c. Lake Texcoco

3. The Aztecs traded goods like **gold, food, and jewelry**.

   a. gold, b. food, c. jewelry

4. The Templo Mayor consisted of **two** main temples. **c. two**

5. The city of Tenochtitlán was built around a large **square**.

   c. square

6. The Aztecs named their capital city **Tenochtitlán**.

   c. Tenochtitlán

7. Tenochtitlán had **more than** fifty thousand residents.

   b. more than

8. The Mexica are often referred to as the **Aztecs**.

   a. Aztecs

9. The Aztec god of the underworld is **Mictlantecutli**.

   c. Mictlantecutli

Chapter 4: The Expansion of the Aztecs

After the Aztecs founded their capital city, they were ready to expand! They continued to increase their power in the Valley of Mexico during the rest of the 1300s. They did this by integrating with other communities. They also expanded through invasion and trade.

The Aztec civilization created a system of governance. A ruler/king (tlatoani) was appointed. A succession *protocol* (procedure) was established. This ensured a new king would *ascend* (rise) to the throne when the old king died.

Acamapichtli was the first official Aztec emperor. Under the leadership of their first huey tlatoani (emperor), the Aztecs advanced their agricultural systems. They produced large amounts of food. It was enough to feed the Aztec people and the rest of the region's population groups!

They traded food across the Basin of Mexico. Their great food supply helped them to increase their authority over more groups of people.

The Aztecs trained their military troops. They were better than most other nearby societies. Their reputation as "fierce warriors" spread, which increased their power throughout the region.

As their strength, influence, and power grew, the Aztecs forced smaller population groups to pay them recurring fees known as tributes. They became wealthier as a result. However, they were not the region's most dominant civilization—at least not yet!

Aztec Mercenaries

The Aztecs provided warriors to the *Tepanec* (teh-pah-nek) nation. Tezozomoc (te-zo-zo-mok) was the ruler of the Tepanec from roughly 1370 until 1426. The Aztecs assisted the Tepanec since they were subjects of the Tepanec. The Aztec rulers Acamapichtli, Huitzilihuitl, and Chimalpopoca cooperated with the Tepanec and provided them with military aid in many wars.

> **Fun Fact**
> " The tribute paid by ancient societies to dominant nations is like the modern "tax" citizens have to pay. "

Picture of Aztec warriors.[10]

The Aztecs helped fight in important battles as mercenaries, or hired warriors. In return, they were given many rewards. Historians think they were paid different kinds of goods to help the Tepanec army. They might have even received land and prisoners taken from the people they helped defeat.

The Aztecs aided the Tepanec in wars against the Toltecs and the Chichimecas. This partnership enabled the Aztec nation to grow its wealth and power.

> **Fun Fact**
> "The Tepanec were an ancient Nahuatl-speaking civilization. They ruled several city-states and tribes in the Basin of Mexico."

However, the Aztecs were still under the dominion of the Tepanec. The Aztecs became bitter about the tribute they were required to pay. They wanted to be more than just subjects of the Tepanec.

Tezozomoc died in 1426. His son, *Tayatzin (tey-at-sin)*, became king. Unfortunately, Tezozomoc's other son, *Maxtla (mahks-tlah)*, forced his way into power. He was a cruel leader. He killed his family members! All this disorder triggered a change in the balance of power in the region.

Tensions in the Basin of Mexico were at an all-time high. The neighboring tribes wanted a change. The Aztecs did too.

The Tepanec War

In 1427, the Tepanec War started. While the war was being fought, Maxtla died. His death at such a crucial point (during a war to maintain dominance) significantly helped the Aztecs to take control.

Fun Fact: The people of Texcoco were known as the *Acolhua (a-cole-wa)*. The people of the ancient city-state Tlacopan were Tepanec. Tlacopan and Texcoco were neighboring tribes in the Valley of Mexico and Tepanec city-states.

Itzcoatl was Tenochtitlán's fourth ruler. He started his reign around the same time the Tepanec War began. He made a risky choice. He agreed to work with Texcoco and Tlacopan to conquer the ruling Tepanec.

Together, the three allies fought a grueling war. Finally, in 1428, the Tepanec were ousted from power!

The Aztec Triple Alliance

This crucial alliance became known as the Aztec Triple Alliance. The Triple Alliance incorporated the ancient city-states of Texcoco, Tlacopan, and Tenochtitlán. The Triple Alliance also captured the Tepanec capital city, *Azcapotzalco (as-cap-ots-al-ko)*.

The Triple Alliance was seen as a force to be reckoned with in the region. The Triple Alliance distributed the Tepanec lands among the three of them.

It is correct to state that when the Triple Alliance was formed, the Aztec Empire began. It was not long before the Aztecs dominated the Triple Alliance. Their army was the biggest and strongest. Their city was the largest and busiest.

Tenochtitlán's king, Itzcoatl, assumed the role of leader within the Triple Alliance. The Triple Alliance moved quickly to integrate the remaining tribes in the Basin of Mexico.

By 1432, the Triple Alliance had taken control of the southern region of the Basin of Mexico. They seized the western region in 1435. By 1440, they had dominated the eastern region.

The Triple Alliance existed until the end of the Aztec Empire in 1521.

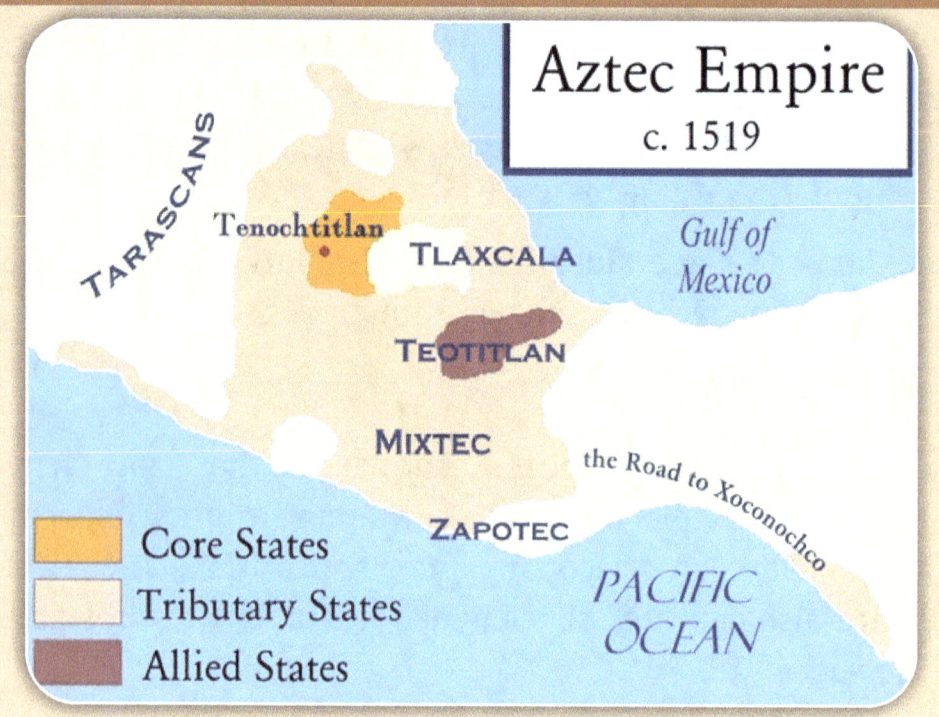

Map representing the Aztec Empire in 1519.[11]

Aztec Rule: Tribute and Aid

Generally, the Aztecs did not destroy cities when they conquered areas or captured cities. In a way, they ruled over tribes with their consent. The Aztecs did not always use brute force and destruction.

The Aztecs let conquered city leaders stay in charge. But there were two rules they had to follow. First, they had to pay tribute twice a year to the Aztecs as a "thank you" for letting them stay in charge. Second, if the Aztecs needed help to fight a battle, they had to send soldiers to fight.

The cities were allowed to partially govern themselves. In return, the Aztecs would help and protect them. They could also trade goods at the Aztec markets and take part in commercial activities within the Aztec Empire.

The Aztec Wars with the Purépecha Empire

The *Purépecha (poo-reh-peh-cha)* Empire resisted Aztec domination in Mexico. Both nations were very powerful in central Mexico. However, their relationship with each other was always strained. They were always at war.

They fought over control of the *Toluca (to-loo-ka)* Valley just west of the Basin of Mexico. These wars were fought between 1455 and 1472. The Aztec Empire managed to press forward slightly.

In 1479, the Purépecha Empire won a significant battle. The victory stopped the Aztec Empire's expansion in the northwest of central Mexico. It was a big blow to the Aztec Empire. The Aztecs never conquered the Purépecha.

Picture of Aztec Jaguar warriors.[12]

The Aztec Wars with the Tlaxcalans

In ancient Mexico, there was a powerful tribe living to the east of Tenochtitlán. These people were called the *Tlaxcalans (tlaks-ka-lan-s)*. The Aztecs shared many cultural characteristics with the Tlaxcalans. They spoke the same language. They even worshiped many of the same gods and had the same religious beliefs and rituals.

Despite this, the two civilizations were arch-rivals. The two waged several wars against each other, including conflicts referred to as flower wars.

"Flower Wars"

The Nahuatl word *xochiyaoyotl (so-chee-ya-yo-yotul)* means "flower war" in English. This word was used by the Aztecs to describe a special kind of war. The goal of these wars was to capture enemy warriors. These captured warriors would be used in religious practices.

Smaller ceremonial armies would fight these battles at a set place on a set day and at a set time. These battles allowed warriors to showcase their fighting abilities. Although these battles involved close combat, they were not one-on-one duels.

Don't worry. We will learn more about the Tlaxcalans in Aztec history in Chapter 9.

The expansion of the Aztecs was an amazing journey. The Mexica went from being a group of nomads to forging one of the greatest empires in Mesoamerica.

In the next chapter, we'll delve into Aztec culture. We'll shed some light on Aztec society, where commerce and creativity thrived!

Chapter 4 Activity

Mark whether the statement is true or false.

Statement	True/ False
1. The Purépecha Empire was a city-state of the Aztec Empire.	
2. The Triple Alliance consisted of three Aztec emperors when it was formed.	
3. The Tepanec War started in 1427.	
4. The Tepanec capital city was overthrown by the Purépecha civilization.	
5. The Triple Alliance included Texcoco, Tlacopan, and Tenochtitlán.	
6. The Aztec emperor during the Tepanec War was Maxtla.	
7. The Aztecs allied with the Tlaxcalans against Tlacopan during the Tepanec War.	
8. The Tlaxcalans moved from Europe to settle in the Gulf of Mexico.	
9. The people of Texcoco were referred to as Acolhua.	
10. The Aztec Empire defeated the Tlaxcalan civilization and owned all their land.	

Chapter 4 Answers

Statement	True/ False
1. The Purépecha Empire was a city-state of the Aztec Empire.	False
2. The Triple Alliance consisted of three Aztec emperors when it was formed.	False
3. The Tepanec War started in 1427.	True
4. The Tepanec capital city was overthrown by the Purépecha civilization.	False
5. The Triple Alliance included Texcoco, Tlacopan, and Tenochtitlán.	True
6. The Aztec emperor during the Tepanec War was Maxtla.	False
7. The Aztecs allied with the Tlaxcalans against Tlacopan during the Tepanec War.	False
8. The Tlaxcalans moved from Europe to settle in the Gulf of Mexico.	False
9. The people of Texcoco were referred to as Acolhua.	True
10. The Aztec Empire defeated the Tlaxcalan civilization and owned all their land.	False

Chapter 5: Aztec Arts, Crafts, and Trade

The Aztec people were experts in many things. They were celebrated for their stunning and creative arts and crafts. From towering statues to delicate jewelry, the Aztecs were true masters.

The Aztec people were also savvy traders. They erected markets that were like giant outdoor shopping malls. These markets were filled with everything from food and clothes to toys and tools. People from all over would come to these marketplaces to trade goods. Their advanced trade networks connected them to societies from far and wide!

Materials Used in Aztec Arts and Crafts

The Aztecs crafted items from materials they gathered locally or gained through trade and territorial expansion. They worked with stone and clay. Precious metals like gold and silver were also transformed into breathtaking artworks and beautiful jewelry by the Aztecs.

They also used coral, copper, pearls, and even feathers and shells. The Aztecs had a fondness for a green gemstone called jade. The Aztecs made fabrics from yucca, maguey, cotton, and wool using various weaving methods. They produced geometric-shaped stamps to make bold imprints on fabrics and other items.

The Aztec people produced goods for daily use, artistic expression, decorative and ceremonial use, and so much more! They created ceramics and stoneware (pottery), paintings, drawings, jewelry, large and small sculpted figures, statues, and unique featherwork art.

Photograph of an Aztec ceramic bowl with a stand. [13]

Aztec Ceramics

The Aztecs produced a variety of ceramic items. The Aztecs crafted ceramics that served practical purposes in daily life. They also created elaborate works of art.

They made items like jugs, plates, cups, and pots. They also made colorful ornaments as decorations for temples and buildings. They made ceramic masks and earrings. They even created musical instruments like ceramic flutes!

Fun Fact

"The Aztecs did not use pottery wheels! Every piece of their pottery was handcrafted."

After handcrafting their pottery pieces, the Aztecs left the items in the sun to dry. The pottery was then kiln-baked. They most likely put the items in pit fires.

The Aztecs decorated their ceramics. They used intricate shapes, designs, and patterns. The Aztecs were able to create a diverse range of patterns by sculpting, illustrating, or engraving the clay. They often drew inspiration from nature for their designs.

A noteworthy Aztec ceramic work of art is the Aztec Sun Stone. It is also called the Calendar Stone. It is a sun-shaped disk that shows the five different sun worlds from Aztec mythology.

The Aztec Sun Stone. [14]

Aztec Featherwork

The Aztecs created many objects using featherwork techniques. Colorful feathers were woven into headwear for their great kings. Feathers were also used to decorate battle shields, cloaks, buildings, temples, and garments.

Feathers carried great meaning in the Aztec religion. Birds were symbolic in the Aztec culture, particularly in religious practices. The Aztecs used feathers from birds like the parrot and hummingbird. The brilliantly colored blue and green feathers of the *Quetzal (kwet-sahl) (bird-type)* were the most cherished.

Aztec Currency and Trade

Trade and agriculture were the pillars of the Aztec economy. The Aztecs used a system of barter trade. This means they swapped items for other items. They did not use modern money. Their currency consisted of the goods they traded. They sometimes traded services too.

Agricultural produce was widely traded. The Aztecs traded corn, squash, hemp, tobacco, peppers, beans, and avocados. They also traded other food, ceramics, fabrics, art, feathers, and metals, such as copper, gold, and silver. They traded gemstones like jade and obsidian. They also traded leather, furs, and animal skins.

The main marketplace in Tenochtitlán, the *Tlatelolco (tla-tel-ohl-ko)*, was the region's *mecca* (hub) of trading activity. Traders came from all over to trade here. There were many marketplaces in Tenochtitlán and the Aztec Empire.

Fun Fact

> The Aztecs used the seeds of cacao trees called cacahuatl (ka-ka-hwua-tul) to make a bitter chocolate drink. The seeds are what we refer to as cocoa beans. The Aztec people believed chocolate was a treasure from the gods. They would grind the beans, add water, and mix it to produce a chocolate drink. They also used cocoa beans for trade.

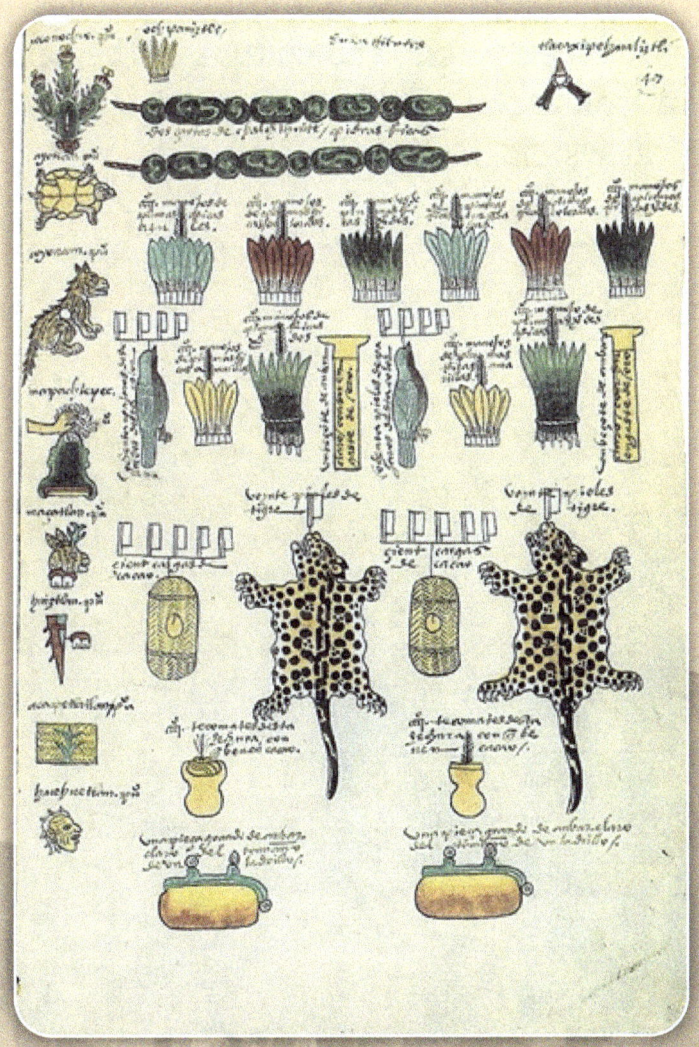

A picture of the various goods the Aztecs used for trade.[15]

Trade was crucial to the Aztec way of life. There was even an elite group of professional traders called the *pochteca (poch-teh-ka)*. The pochteca traveled near and far! They would bring their finds back to the Aztec capital.

> **Fun Fact**
> " Given their wide-ranging travels and vast knowledge of many areas, pochteca were sometimes used as spies! "

Aztec arts and crafts are enduring symbols of their admiration for beauty, skill, and culture. In the next chapter, we'll take a look at the inner workings of Aztec society and their political systems.

Chapter 5 Activity

Answer the questions listed below.

1. What were five goods the Aztecs used to trade?
2. Did the Aztecs use pottery wheels?
3. How did the Aztecs create pottery pieces?
4. What was the name of the elite traders in Aztec society?
5. What are three items the Aztecs created using feathers?
6. How did the Aztecs make their chocolate drink?
7. What was the main marketplace in Tenochtitlán called?

Chapter 5 Answers

1. What were five goods the Aztecs used to trade? **Corn, feathers, food, gold, copper, jade, jewelry, pottery, fabric, obsidian, chili, cacao seeds, avocados, squash.**

2. Did the Aztecs use pottery wheels? **No.**

3. How did the Aztecs create pottery pieces? **The Aztecs molded clay with their hands. They left the items in the sun to dry. Once dry, the pieces were kiln-baked. The Aztecs would decorate the pottery with creative and colorful designs.**

4. What was the name of the elite traders in Aztec society? **Pochteca.**

5. What are three items the Aztecs created using feathers? **Headwear, battle shields, and cloaks.**

6. How did the Aztecs make their chocolate drink? **The Aztecs would grind cocoa beans into powder form, add some water, and mix this to make a chocolate drink.**

7. What was the main marketplace in Tenochtitlán called? **Tlatelolco.**

Chapter 6: Aztec Society and Political Organization

Society refers to the way people live together as a large group. Politics refers to how decisions and rules are made for people to follow. The Aztecs were ahead of their time in the way they structured their society and politics.

Aztec Society's Structure

Aztec society had a clear hierarchy. This means the Aztecs were put into classes from highest to lowest importance. Each class had a role to play. Imagine a pyramid with layers. Each layer is a different category/class group of Aztec people, ranked from highest to lowest.

In Aztec society, a person's social class was the same as their parents. It was difficult to move to a higher-ranking social group.

Let's look at the different classes.

Aztec Emperor

The *huey (hoo-ee-y) tlatoani (tla-to-aa-ne)* ("great speaker") was the emperor of the Aztec Empire. He lived in the capital city, Tenochtitlán. He had the highest position in the empire.

A picture of Montezuma I (the fifth emperor of the Aztec Empire). [16]

> **Fun Fact**
>
> The Aztecs believed the emperor had been chosen by the gods to be their ruler! The huey tlatoani even had the power to decide when the Aztec Empire would go to war.
>
> Every city-state had a tlatoani. Each tlatoani had to obey the emperor's orders. So, the emperor was the king of kings in the Aztec world!

> **Fun Fact**
>
> Just below the emperor was the cihuacoatl (see-wah-ko-atul). The cihuacoatl controlled the internal affairs of the Aztec capital. It was the second-most important position in the city of Tenochtitlán.

Aztec Noblemen

Aztec noblemen and royalty held high-ranking positions in Aztec society and government. They had special rights and benefits. They were regarded as more important than most of the classes in the Aztec hierarchy.

The nobles often acted as judges. They ensured peace and order in the Aztec Empire. They also controlled and managed tributes. The nobles provided the king with resources, financial assistance, and military troops. They were advisors to the emperor and assisted him in making decisions.

Aztec noblemen played vital roles in maintaining the social and political order in the Aztec Empire. The nobles owned a large amount of land. They employed commoners to work on their land and grow crops. This gave them authority over the lower classes. The workers would receive a safe place to stay and jobs. In return, they would give tribute to the nobles.

Nobles also included the following groups:

- Elite warriors, such as the Eagle Warriors and the Jaguar Warriors, were key to the Aztec Empire's success. They were nobles, so they were given land and power. Ordinary people could work their way into the noble class by proving themselves during battles. This was a very difficult process. Few succeeded. This was because many nobles were excellent warriors. It was a great honor to be an elite warrior in the Aztec Empire.

- Priests, called *tlamacazqui (tla-ma-kas-kwee)*, were very important in Aztec society. The Aztec religion was a fundamental part of the Aztec civilization, so priests were equal to noblemen. Priests did not have to be born into a noble family. Someone of a lower rank could gain entry to the special school for priests. Only gifted students from lower classes were chosen for the priesthood. Schooling and training were intense. Priests had many religious duties and roles.

- Military leaders (generals), important people in the government, and people who created laws were also classed as noblemen.

Fun Fact

" The pochteca (elite traders) were not part of the noble class. However, they could become as wealthy as the nobility. They could not gain noble social status, though. "

Macehualtin Class (Commoners)

The *macehualtin (ma-se-hwal-tin)* formed the largest class of people in Aztec society. They were the ordinary (common) people.

The macehualtin were mostly farmers, artisans, and traders. They had to fight in wars and battles. They also worked as builders and performed manual labor. They would be called upon to build temples and roads when work needed to be done.

A photograph of the Tlatelolco roads in modern Mexico City. [17]

Mayeque Class

The *mayeque (may-e-kwe)* was one of the lowest classes in Aztec society. They did not own land of their own. Typically, they farmed parts of land on large farms owned by wealthy Aztec families. The mayeque would have to give some of what they grew to the owner as payment for using his land.

Tlacotin Class

The lowest class in Aztec society was slaves. They were called *tlacotin (tla-co-teen)*. This group was made up of war prisoners and criminals who had committed serious crimes. People who had debts they couldn't pay back sometimes sold themselves as slaves.

Slaves were owned by higher-ranking classes and could not own land. People who were born into the tlacotin class were part of the mayeque class at birth.

> **Fun Fact**
>
> "Slaves had a chance to gain their freedom. When their owner died, a slave who had worked very hard could be set free. But if the slave was not set free, the slave would be sold to a new owner or go to the next of kin."

The Family Unit and Education in Aztec Society

In Aztec society, marriage was viewed as a bond between individuals, entire families, and sometimes even political groups. Men were able to have many wives. They would have one "primary" wife. Only the children from the primary wife could inherit.

Aztec women were allowed to do far more than just chores! Women participated in trade. They could own land and make contributions to religious practices. Women were regarded as equals in Aztec society.

As time went on, Aztec society focused more on male domination and warfare. This led to a less prominent role for women. Their focus shifted more to having children and doing domestic tasks.

Education was *compulsory* (required) for Aztec children of all social classes. The school for noble kids was called *calmecac (kal-mek-ak)*. The children learned about astronomy, theology, and art. Some commoners were chosen to attend the elite school to study and become members of the priesthood.

Commoners went to a school called *telpochcalli (tehl-poch-cahl-lee)*. The children were taught morals, physical training, and practical trades. Children who excelled in classes, such as combat training, were given a chance to move up in class status.

The Aztec Empire's Government

The capital, Tenochtitlán, was the headquarters of the Aztec Empire's governing body. The emperor was the head of government and the empire. Each city-state in the Aztec Empire was an *altepetl (al-tee-pe-tul)*.

Each altepetl had a tlatoani to oversee government, military, and economic affairs. Each king could govern with a degree of self-rule if they followed the rules of the Tenochtitlán government. They had to pay the required tribute to the Aztec capital city.

The altepetl was subdivided into *calpulli (kah-l-pull-i)*, small rural communities where commoners lived and worked together. These communities were organized and governed by local leaders (chiefs) and paid tribute. Each calpulli decided how the land would be used.

We have now learned that the bedrock of the Aztec civilization was their organized society and government. Next, let's learn more about the fascinating Aztec religion!

Chapter 6 Activity

Fill in the correct word in the blank spaces provided in the sentences below.

1. The most powerful person in the Aztec Empire was the emperor. In Nahuatl, he was called _____.

2. The slave class in Aztec society was referred to as _____.

3. The noble class included _____.

4. The city-states in the Aztec Empire were called the _____.

5. Small rural communities inhabited by Aztec commoners were referred to as _____.

6. The commoners were referred to as the _____.

Chapter 6 Answers

1. The most powerful person in the Aztec Empire was the emperor. In Nahuatl, he was called **Huey Tlatoani**.

2. The slave class in Aztec society was referred to as **tlacotin**.

3. The noble class included **priests, Eagle Warriors, and Jaguar Warriors**.

4. The city-states in the Aztec Empire were called the **altepetl**.

5. Small rural communities inhabited by Aztec commoners were referred to as **calpulli**.

6. The commoners were referred to as the **macehualtin**.

Chapter 7: Aztec Religion and Deities

The Aztec religion is another cornerstone of this complex civilization. The Aztecs worshiped *deities (deey-a-tees)* (gods).

The Aztec religion was *syncretistic (sin-cret-is-tic)*. This means the Aztec civilization took elements from other Mesoamerican cultures and incorporated them into their religion. The Aztec religion was so important that it influenced people's everyday life, cultural practices, and societal norms.

The Aztec civilization believed in and worshiped a *pantheon* (collection/group) of deities. Let's look at some of their most popular gods!

Huitzilopochtli

Huitzilopochtli (wee-tsee-loh-pohch-tlee) was the god of the sun and war. The Aztecs believed he guided them to find the place where they settled and created their capital city.

People believed Huitzilopochtli had a special connection to fire. His main weapon was called Xiuhcoatl *(see-uh-ko-atul)*, which means "fire serpent" in the Aztec language, Nahuatl. It looked like a snake made of fire and was very powerful. Huitzilopochtli used Xiuhcoatl to fight his enemies and protect the world.

Some people also connected Xiuhcoatl to another fire god named Xiuhtecuhtli *(shoo-teh-coot-lee)*, but Xiuhcoatl wasn't exactly a spirit or version of that god. It was more like a magical fire snake that the gods could use in battle.

The Aztecs believed the spirits of their fallen warriors came back to the earthly *realm* (land) as hummingbirds. These brave fallen soldiers and women who lost their lives during childbirth were part of Huitzilopochtli's exclusive group of helpers.

A picture of Huitzilopochtli.[18]

Fun Fact

> Huitzilopochtli is derived from a combination of two Nahuatl words. The word huitzilin (wiy-tsiy-lihn) means "hummingbird." The word opochtli (op-och-tu-lee) means "left."

Tezcatlipoca

Tezcatlipoca (tess-kaht-li-poh-kah) was the deity of conflict, hurricanes, the night sky, and obsidian. He and his three brothers were born to a *primordial dual god* (a god that has existed since the start of time and is made up of two different sides). This god was called *Ometecuhtli (ome-te-koot-lee)* or *Omecihuatl (ome-ki-wua-tul)*.

Fun Fact

> The Aztecs believed every person shared a deep connection with some type of animal. They also believed they could change into this animal to hide their human appearance. This belief is known as nagualism (na-goo-a-liz-m). The animal disguise is known as a nagual (na-goo-al).

A picture of the Aztec god, Tezcatlipoca. [19]

Tezcatlipoca's nagual was a jaguar. He is frequently shown in Aztec art as a jaguar with a line of black paint on his face and a shiny black obsidian mirror as one of his feet.

The Aztecs believed his role was to protect the slave class. The slaves were his children. The Aztecs believed that slave owners who treated their slaves poorly would suffer at the hands of Tezcatlipoca.

Quetzalcoatl

Quetzalcoatl **(ket-sahl-koh-ah-tul)** was an important Aztec god. The Aztecs believed he was the god of life and wisdom. He was also the Aztec god of day and light and elements of nature like the wind and rain. He was directly connected to Aztec arts and crafts. He was also believed to be the founding god of Aztec priests.

A picture of the Aztec god Quetzalcoatl. [20]

The Aztecs believed that Quetzalcoatl represented death and rebirth. He was the evening and morning star (the planet Venus). Quetzalcoatl was thought to be the creator of calendars and books. He was seen as the guardian of artisans and tradespeople.

In Aztec *mythology* (a collection of legends and folk stories), Quetzalcoatl collected the bones of ancient dead people in *Mictlan (me-k-tul-ahn)* (the underworld). He mixed a small amount of his godly blood with these bones and created the people of the present universe.

Xipe Totec

Xipe Totec (zi-pey toe-tek) was the founding god of seeds and plants, goldsmiths, and gemstone artisans. The Aztecs believed he was the supreme force of the east, the earth, the seasons, agriculture, freedom, and warfare.

He was named Xipe Totec because he *flayed* (whipped) his body. This act provided humankind with food to eat. His act of harming himself to benefit people was believed to be shown in events that happen in nature. For example, a snake sheds its old skin to reveal a fresh layer beneath.

Aztec Religious Rituals

Religious practices were an important part of Aztec life. Religious ceremonies took place in homes, temples, and communal gathering areas. These ceremonies could be daily, monthly, or yearly events. They were carefully scheduled to line up with events in astronomy and the cycles of nature.

The Aztecs performed rituals mostly to honor their gods. Ceremonies usually involved offerings and sacrifices to their deities. There was also music, dance, and food.

The Aztecs sacrificed a wide range of items, such as food, jewelry, gemstones, and different animals. The Aztecs also made human sacrifices to *appease* (satisfy) their gods. They sacrificed prisoners they had captured during wars with enemy tribes. The Aztecs believed human sacrifices were necessary to ensure balance and order in the world.

The Templo Mayor

The Templo Mayor is the most well-known Aztec temple. The temple was used for religious worship and to make offerings to the gods.

This structure was built as a dual temple to honor Huitzilopochtli and the god of rain and fertility, *Tlaloc (tla-lohk)*. Each god had a sanctuary at the top of the pyramid. There was a separate staircase to access each one.

Pyramids of the Sun and the Moon

The Pyramids of the Sun and the Moon are located in the ancient city of Teotihuacan. They were built before the time of the Aztecs, but they were used by the Aztecs as sacred temples. They were named by the Aztecs to honor the god of rain, Tlaloc, and the god of the moon, *Chalchiuhtlicue (Chal-chee-hwee-tul-ee-kway)*.

The Pyramid of the Sun is in the center of the Causeway of the Dead, which was the main road through the center of Teotihuacan. It was called this because it was believed the dead traveled this road on their way to the afterlife. The Pyramid of the Sun was purposefully positioned between the Citadel (a large square courtyard at the beginning of the Causeway of the Dead) to its south and the Pyramid of the Moon to its north.

Tonalpohualli: The Aztec Religious Calendar

The Aztec civilization had a very special calendar named the *tonalpohualli* **(toh-nahl-poh-wah-lee)** ("count of days"), which they inherited from their predecessors. This calendar was used by several Mesoamerican civilizations, including the *Maya (my-yah)* and the Olmecs. The tonalpohualli was used by the Aztecs to forecast the weather and set dates for religious rituals.

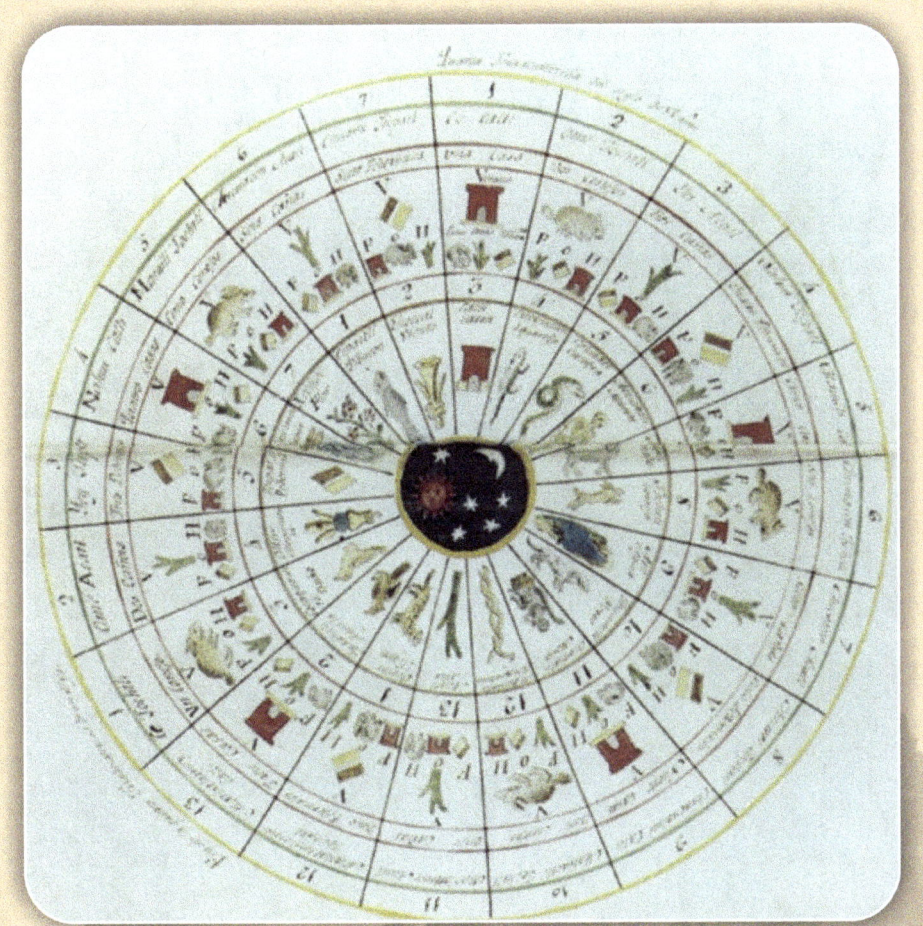

A picture of the Aztec tonalpohualli calendar.[21]

Chapter 7 Activity

Answer the questions listed below.

1. Was religion an important part of Aztec culture?
2. What are the names of two important Aztec religious buildings?
3. What are the names of two of the most prominent Aztec deities?
4. Did the Aztec religion incorporate elements from other Mesoamerican religions?
5. Did the Aztecs have a religious calendar? If so, what was it called?

Chapter 7 Answers

1. Was religion an important part of Aztec culture? **Yes.**

2. What are the names of two important Aztec religious buildings? **The Templo Mayor, the Pyramid of the Sun, the Pyramid of the Moon.**

3. What are the names of two of the most prominent Aztec deities? **Xipe Totec, Quetzalcoatl, Tezcatlipoca, Huitzilopochtli, Tlaloc, or Chalchiuhtlicue.**

4. Did the Aztec religion incorporate elements from other Mesoamerican religions? **Yes.**

5. Did the Aztecs have a religious calendar? If so, what is it referred to? **Yes, the Aztec religious calendar is known as the tonalpohualli.**

Chapter 8: A Day in the Life of the Aztecs

Are you wondering what a day in the life of an Aztec was like? Their days were filled with routines and work. Schools were packed with children. The fields and farms were active. The cities and marketplaces were buzzing with people.

Let's take a look at a typical day for an Aztec!

Morning Rituals

Aztec families woke up early. They looked at the morning star, a symbol of their sun god, and said morning prayers. They took note of the day's number and sign on their calendars. This gave them insight into what the day would be like.

Hygiene and staying clean were important in Aztec society. They cleaned their homes and took a morning bath.

It is believed the Aztecs started their daily activities before they had their morning meal. The men would farm, make items, build structures or roads, trade at the market, or fight in wars.

Boys went with their fathers to assist them and learn about the work they did. Women did household chores. They stitched, sewed, weaved, and made crafts. Girls would assist them and learn how to do these tasks.

The family came together a little later for their breakfast meal. They would enjoy a hearty maize porridge or tortillas. Toppings were usually honey, chili, or a sauce with beans.

After breakfast, the men and women would return to doing their work. The children would go to school.

Afternoon Meal

The Aztecs took a break from their daily activities in the afternoon. They enjoyed a hearty meal. Lunch, called *icacalatl (e-ka-ka-lah-tul)*, was the main meal of the day. It was generally a nutritious stew made with legumes and vegetables. They also might enjoy tortillas or tamales filled/topped with squash, beans, and tomatoes. When available, they would have meat or fish.

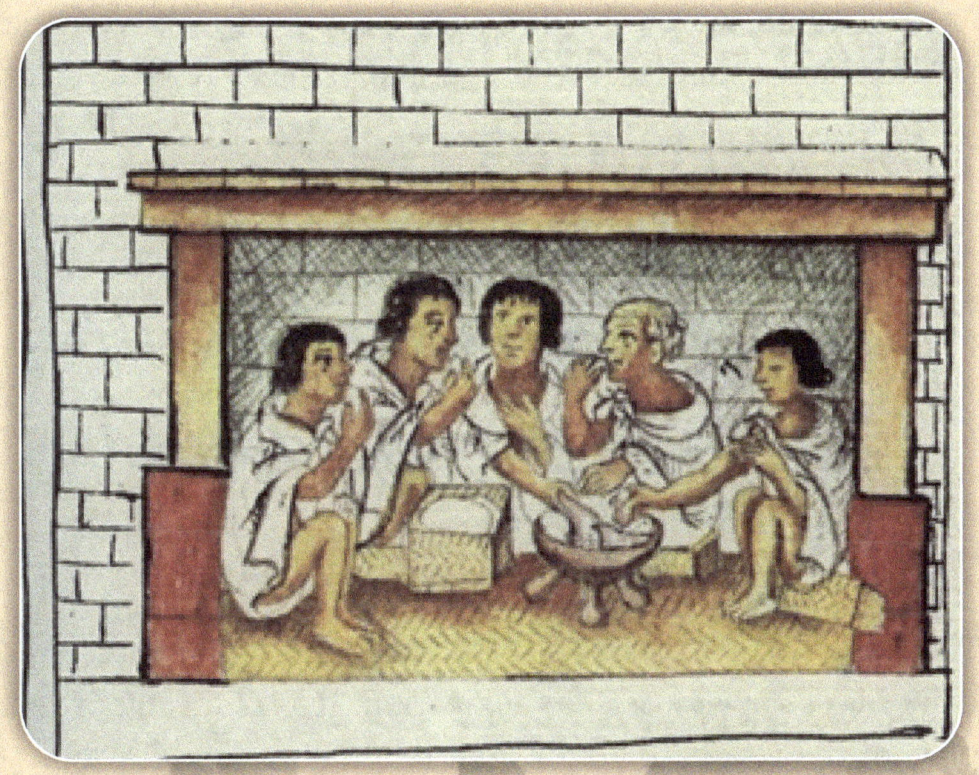

A picture depicting Aztec men sharing a meal.[22]

After they had lunch, they would continue with their work or education. Later in the afternoon and evening, they might play games and activities.

Aztec Clothing

The Aztecs' clothing was based on their social rank. Commoners wore plain and practical clothing most of the time. The noble class did too, but their clothes were flashier than the commoners. They wore accessories that the lower classes were not allowed to wear.

Male nobles and commoners wore a *loincloth* (a simple garment covering the waist). This was worn with a cloak. Aztec women wore a blouse with a long skirt. Aztec male nobles wore simple leather sandals. Most Aztecs went barefoot.

Fun Fact

> Everybody in Aztec society had to be barefoot when entering a temple. Nobody was allowed to wear footwear in the presence of the emperor. This was considered a way to respect the Aztec Empire's ruler.

Aztec Poetry, Music, and Dance

The Aztecs incorporated poetry, song, and dance into their daily lives. It was used for relaxation. It was an important way for the Aztecs to honor their religion in everyday life.

The Aztecs used different musical instruments. They crafted these instruments from eggshells, clay, wood, and other materials. They made flutes, drums, and shakers.

They would also chant songs and dance. Aztecs would sing as they worked and during their leisure activities.

Aztec stories and legends would be taught and shared at gatherings. At the end of a full day, the Aztecs would spend some time with their family and then go to bed.

A picture of Aztecs dancing and singing with musical instruments.[23]

Aztec Ceremonies, Festivals, and Celebrations

The Aztecs frequently celebrated special occasions. Religious ceremonies were arranged throughout the Aztec year, mostly to honor the gods. The Aztecs dressed in costumes and accessories for their festivals. Their outfits depended on their social class.

FUN FACT

> The Aztecs undertook the New Fire Ceremony every fifty-two years. Another important celebration was the Rain Festival, which honored the Aztec god Tlaloc. The Aztecs offered prayers and sacrifices so that Tlaloc would provide rain for the crops to grow.

A picture of the Aztecs performing a ritual during a ceremony for rain. [24]

Chapter 8 Activity

Mark whether the statement in column A is true or false in column B.

Column A: Statement	Column B: True/ False
1. The Aztecs did not eat breakfast.	
2. The Aztecs observed a morning religious ritual related to their sun god.	
3. The main daily meal of the Aztecs was their afternoon meal, known as icacalatl in Nahuatl.	
4. The Aztec children played games all day and were only educated when they were twenty years old.	
5. The Aztecs used poetry in their daily lives.	
6. The Aztecs made music with instruments like drums and flutes.	
7. The Aztecs had several religious ceremonies throughout the year.	
8. The Aztecs only used clay to make their musical instruments.	
9. The Aztecs were untidy and did not clean their homes.	

Chapter 8 Answers

Column A: Statement	Column B: True/ False
1. The Aztecs did not eat breakfast.	False
2. The Aztecs observed a morning religious ritual related to their sun god.	True
3. The main daily meal of the Aztecs was their afternoon meal, known as icacalatl in Nahuatl.	True
4. The Aztec children played games all day and were only educated when they were twenty years old.	False
5. The Aztecs used poetry in their daily lives.	True
6. The Aztecs made music with instruments like drums and flutes.	True
7. The Aztecs had several religious ceremonies throughout the year.	True
8. The Aztecs only used clay to make their musical instruments.	False
9. The Aztecs were untidy and did not clean their homes.	False

Chapter 9: The Spanish Conquest

In this chapter, we focus on the arrival of the Spaniards. Let's take a look at the conflicts that happened and their impact on the Aztec civilization.

The Arrival of the Spaniards

Before the arrival of the Spanish, tensions existed between the ruling Aztec Empire and other tribes, such as the Tlaxcalans.

In 1519, the Aztec emperor was *Montezuma (mon-teh-zoo-mah)* II. Hernán Cortés commanded the Spanish *conquistadors (kuhn-kee-stuh-dorz)* (soldiers) who arrived on ships in the Gulf of Mexico that year.

The first contact between the Spaniards and the Aztecs was not violent. The Aztecs were unsure about the Spanish, but they tried to understand who these strangers were and why they were there. They did not view the conquistadors as enemies.

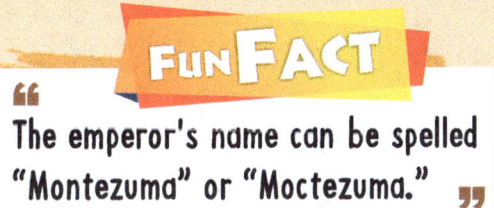

Fun Fact: "The emperor's name can be spelled "Montezuma" or "Moctezuma.""

After the Spanish arrived in 1519, they started gaining control of the region through invasion or by arranging *coalitions* (partnerships) with existing tribes.

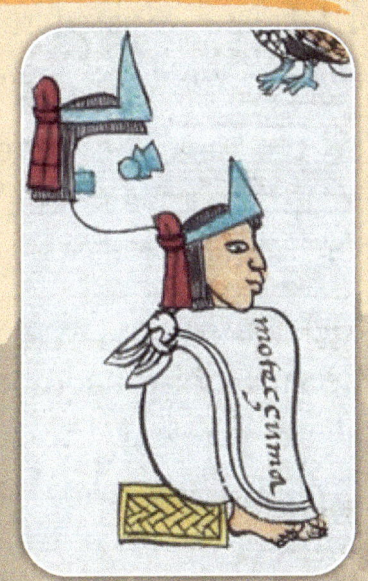

A picture of Montezuma II from the Codex Mendoza.[25]

Fun Fact

> The Aztecs believed that the god Quetzalcoatl might return during a special year in their calendar called 1 Reed, the first year in their fifty-two-year cycle. It's not clear if they thought he would return every time that year came or just once. The year 1519 was a 1 Reed year, which made it feel important. Some people later said the Aztecs thought Cortés might be Quetzalcoatl. However, many historians today aren't sure if that's true. We may never really know.

The Tlaxcalans and the Spanish against the Aztec Empire

The Aztecs had tried to conquer the *Tlaxcalans (tlaks-kal-ans)* several times. After the Spaniards arrived in 1519, the Tlaxcalans resisted them. They soon realized the Spanish soldiers were too powerful for them.

So, the Tlaxcalans opted to help the Spaniards conquer their long-time rivals, the Aztecs. They provided them with shelter and food.

The Tlaxcalans were extremely useful to the Spaniards. Because they had fought against the Aztecs, they knew about the way the Aztecs fought. They also had tactical insight into the land. The Tlaxcalans provided the Spaniards with thousands of trained, skilled warriors.

A picture of the Spaniards and their allies fighting together to overthrow the Aztecs.[26]

The Spaniards entered Tenochtitlán on November 8th, 1519. Hernán Cortés took Montezuma II prisoner. There was tension between the Spaniards and the Aztecs in Tenochtitlán.

The Toxcatl Festival and Massacre

The Spaniards agreed to allow the Aztecs to go ahead with their important religious Festival of *Toxcatl (tohsh-kah-tul)*. Hernán Cortés was away during the festival. The festival took place on May 20th, 1520. The Aztecs invited the conquistadors to attend as guests. Hernán Cortés was away during the festival.

During the festival, Pedro de Alvarado led Spanish soldiers in an attack on the Aztecs in Tenochtitlán. Several Aztec noblemen were killed, and the festival turned into a bloody and violent event. This event became known as the Toxcatl Massacre. The Spaniards were forced out of Tenochtitlán and went to regroup at their base camp in the Tlaxcalan settlement.

There are different stories of the events that happened to Montezuma II after he was captured. Some believe the Aztecs killed Montezuma because he cooperated with the Spanish. They wanted his brother to rule instead. Others believe he was tortured and killed by the Spaniards.

Emperor Montezuma II died in captivity on June 30th, 1520. The next ruler was Montezuma II's brother, *Cuitlahuac (kwi-tla-wak)*.

The Fall of Tenochtitlán

The Spanish were aided by the Tlaxcalans and other native tribes. Many were upset about the Aztec rule. They didn't like paying tributes. They also didn't want to be sacrificed at Aztec temples.

The Spanish and their allies attacked Tenochtitlán. They entered the city on May 22nd, 1521. They encircled the city to close it off. They also battled against the Aztecs within the city. After almost three months, the Spanish took charge of the city on August 13th, 1521. Most of Tenochtitlán was destroyed, and the Aztec Empire was basically ruined.

The Last Aztec Emperor

The last emperor of the Aztec Empire was *Cuauhtémoc (kwa-wa-te-mok)*. Cuauhtémoc was opposed to Spanish rule. He led the Aztecs against the conquistadors in the capital city.

Cuauhtémoc was captured by the Spaniards when he tried to escape Tenochtitlán in August 1521. After he was captured, he was treated like any other prisoner. He was tortured for information about the location of Aztec riches. It is believed that he did not give the conquistadors any information and remained loyal to the Aztec Empire. He was killed on February 28th, 1525.

A photograph of a statue of the last Aztec emperor, Cuauhtémoc.[27]

Key Factors for the Spanish Conquistadors' Victory over the Aztec Empire

Several factors led to the Aztec Empire's defeat by the Spaniards. The main factors include the following:

- **Superior weaponry:** The conquistadors used steel weapons (swords, spears, cannons, and an early type of gun called a *harquebus (hark-we-bus)*. They also had metal armor. The Aztecs had stone, bronze, and wood weapons at their disposal. The Aztecs were not familiar with the sound of a cannon firing. This frightened and confused them.

- **Native tribe alliances:** The local native tribes joined the conquistadors. Local tribes fought with the Spanish. They also provided the Spanish with information about the Aztecs' war tactics and the local environment.

- **Smallpox epidemic:** The Spanish brought European diseases with them. The smallpox disease was devastating. The Aztec population had not been exposed to this disease before. Many Aztecs became very ill, and many died. This made it easier for the Spaniards to take over.

During the rest of the 16th century, the Spanish charged through the rest of central and southern Mexico. They occupied and settled in the region.

After the Spanish defeated the Aztecs, they renamed the land New Spain. This was the start of the Spanish colonial period—a time when Spain controlled much of Mexico and other parts of the Americas. This period lasted for about three hundred years. Eventually, the people in those places fought for and won their independence.

A 19th-century engraving from an original portrait of Hernán Cortés. [28]

The fall of the Aztec Empire was a key moment in the history of Mesoamerica. In the final chapter of our book, we reflect on the legacy of the Aztec Empire.

Chapter 9 Activity

Insert the correct answer from the options provided for each of the following sentences.

1. The Spanish arrived in the Basin of Mexico in _____.

    a. 1519,   b. 1520,   c. 1510.

2. The Spaniards captured the Aztec emperor called _____.

    a. Montezuma II,   b. Montezuma I,   c. Itzcoatl.

3. The Spanish conquistadors brought a disease called _____ to the Gulf of Mexico from Europe.

    a. flu,   b. smallpox,   c. cancer.

4. The last emperor of the Aztec Empire was _____.

    a. Montezuma II,   b. Cuitlahuac,   c. Cuauhtémoc.

5. The Spanish renamed the captured Aztec land _____.

    a. New Spain,   b. Spanish conquest,   c. New Europe.

Chapter 9 Answers

1. The Spanish arrived in the Basin of Mexico in 1519.

   a. 1519

2. The Spaniards captured the Aztec emperor Montezuma II.

   a. Montezuma II

3. The Spanish conquistadors brought a disease called smallpox to the Gulf of Mexico from Europe.

   b. smallpox

4. The last emperor of the Aztec Empire was Cuauhtémoc.

   c. Cuauhtémoc

5. The Spanish renamed the captured Aztec land New Spain.

   c. New Spain

Chapter 10: Legacy of the Aztec Empire

Even though the Aztec civilization fell centuries ago, its influence can be seen in Mexico's culture, society, and politics today. Let's read about the lasting impact of the Aztec Empire.

Moctezuma metro station in modern Mexico City.[29]

Aztec Codices

The Aztecs kept written records. These records are referred to as codices. Unfortunately, the codices produced by the Aztecs before the Spaniards arrived were destroyed by the Spanish conquistadors.

Several other Aztec codices detailing important Aztec information were written after the Spaniards arrived in Mexico. They were written during the 16th century with key details about Aztec religious rituals, astronomy, and history.

These codices include the Codex Badiano, Codex Borgia, Codex Mendoza, and the Florentine Codex. The codices have been studied by historians and provide valuable insight into Aztec culture and history. These surviving Aztec codices have been preserved and are kept in museums and libraries in Mexico and throughout the world.

Aztec Language

Nahuatl, the language of the Aztecs, influences the language used in Mexico and other parts of the world today. *Contemporary* (modern) Mexican Spanish incorporates various words, phrases, and derivations from the Nahuatl language.

There are many words and phrases in Spanish (and even some in English) that remind us of how important the Aztecs have been in shaping modern languages.

A picture of the Templo Mayor ruins in modern Mexico. [30]

Aztec Architecture and Art

Aztec architecture has inspired structures, monuments, and buildings in modern Mexico. Some modern Mexican towns are designed like Aztec cities, featuring a main square in the center with roads leading out from it. Mexico City is built on ancient Tenochtitlán, and the city's layout reflects the urban planning the Aztecs used.

The famous modern Mexican architect, Mario Pani's design of the UNAM Campus displays Aztec-inspired symmetry in its layout and buildings. (The UNAM Campus is the National Autonomous University of Mexico.)

Building materials the Aztecs used (such as adobe and stone) are often used during the construction of modern Mexican buildings.

The enduring impact of the Aztecs is further highlighted in Mexican modern art and crafts. Modern Mexican textiles, murals, pottery, and other ceramic artworks use symbolism, geometric patterns, and vibrant colors that were typically used by the Aztecs.

Aztec Agriculture and Food

The Aztecs were master farmers. They used groundbreaking techniques like the chinampas or "floating gardens." We talked about these earlier in the book, but in case you forgot, they are manmade pieces of land built on water. They were used for farming and gardening. Aztec practices continue to inspire modern sustainable farming and urban gardening projects.

However, the Aztecs' influence did not stop with farming methods. The Aztecs also introduced Europeans to a variety of crops. They farmed crops like maize, beans, and squash, which are staples of the modern Mexican diet and enjoyed across the world.

Aztec Heritage in Modern Mexico City

Mexicans continue to honor and preserve the Aztec legacy. Several places and monuments exist in Mexico City that honor the Aztec civilization.

The Templo Mayor Museum and the National Museum of Anthropology have impressive collections of Aztec artifacts. Some of the items on display include Aztec pottery, statues, and sculptures. These items show us how the Aztecs lived, what they believed in, and how skilled they were at making things. Their detailed stonework and jewelry show us how much the Aztecs respected nature and their gods.

Mexico's coat of arms.[31]

The Aztec culture even influenced modern Mexico's coat of arms. This symbol is even on the national flag. It shows an eagle devouring a snake while sitting on a cactus. This comes from the legend about the founding of Tenochtitlán.

The coat of arms is a daily reminder of Mexico's Aztec history. It shows how the history of the Aztecs and Mexico remains connected.

Conclusion

It is time to conclude our exploration of the Aztec civilization. We have zoomed through time and taken a close look at the world of the Aztecs. We have looked at their humble beginnings as the Mexica, their remarkable achievements, and their continued legacy in Mexico and other parts of the world.

We hope this book has inspired you to journey through many more pages of history. Enjoy your future history adventures!

Chapter 10 Activity

Complete the Aztec timeline below. Enter an event from Aztec history in column B that corresponds with the relevant year in column A.

Column A: Date	Column B: Description of events in Aztec history
1100 CE	
1325 CE	
1427 CE	
1428 CE	
1502 CE	
1519 CE	
1521 CE	

Chapter 10 Answers

Column A: Date	Column B: Description of events in Aztec history
1100 CE	Around this time, the Mexica/Aztecs left their homeland, Aztlan, to search for another place to settle. They traveled south toward central Mexico.
1325 CE	The Aztecs founded their capital, Tenochtitlán.
1427 CE	Itzcoatl became the fourth emperor of the Aztecs.
1428 CE	The Triple Alliance was formed. This event marked the beginning of the Aztec Empire.
1502 CE	Montezuma II became the emperor of the Aztec Empire.
1519 CE	The Spanish conquistadors arrived in the Valley of Mexico.
1521 CE	The Spaniards defeated the Aztecs and took control of their capital city, Tenochtitlán.

If you want to learn more about tons of other exciting historical periods, check out our other books!

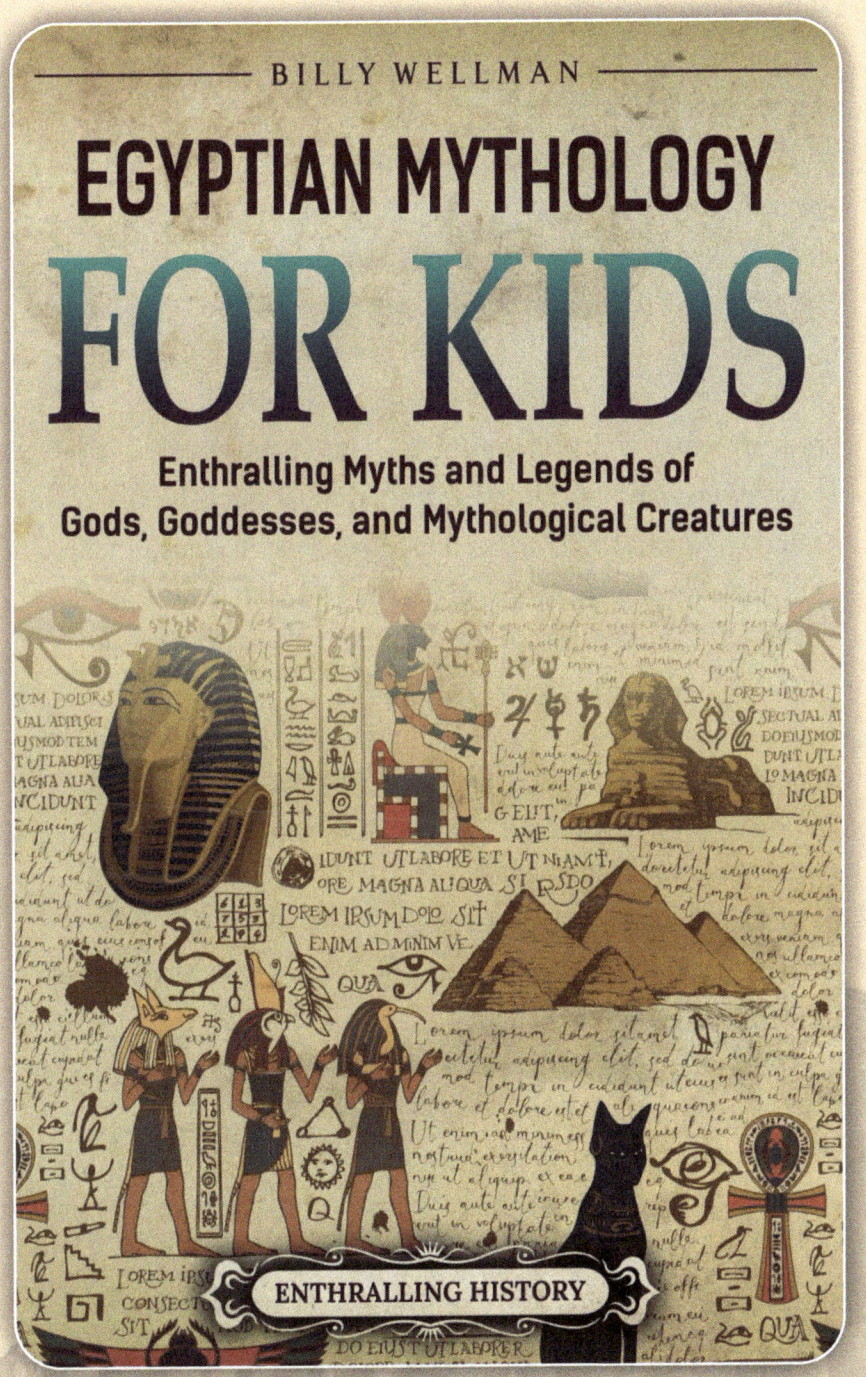

Bibliography

The following websites were accessed for relevant information on the Aztecs during January 2024:

- https://education.nationalgeographic.org/resource/aztec-civilization/
- https://www.britannica.com/topic/Aztec
- https://www.history.com/topics/ancient-americas/aztecs
- https://www.worldhistory.org/article/845/aztec-society/
- https://www.britannica.com/topic/Aztec-religion
- https://www.thoughtco.com/things-to-know-about-the-aztecs-170043
- https://www.worldhistory.org/Aztec_Civilization/
- https://www.historyhit.com/facts-about-aztec-empire/
- https://www.thoughtco.com/aztec-triple-alliance-170036
- https://www.historycrunch.com/aztec-triple-alliance.html#/
- https://www.khanacademy.org/humanities/art-americas/early-cultures/aztec-mexica/a/introduction-to-the-aztecs-mexica
- https://www.worldhistory.org/Ehecatl/
- https://www.britannica.com/summary/Key-People-of-the-Aztec-Empire

If you're looking for additional information about the Aztec civilization, check out these great resources.

Awesome Books for Kids about the Aztecs:

- de Las Casas, Dianne. Blue Frog: The Legend of Chocolate. Pelican Publishing Company, Inc. 2011.
- McDermott, Gerald. Musicians of the Sun. Simon & Schuster Books for Young Readers. 1997.

Great Websites for Kids about the Aztecs:

- https://kids.nationalgeographic.com/history/article/aztec-civilization
- https://kids.britannica.com/kids/article/Aztec/352810
- https://historyforkids.org/the-aztecs-facts-information-for-kids-2/
- https://kids.britannica.com/kids/article/Tenochtitlán/627438

- https://kids.britannica.com/kids/article/Montezuma-II/544227
- https://kids.kiddle.co/Itzcoatl
- https://study.com/academy/lesson/aztec-hierarchy-lesson-for-kids.html
- https://historyforkids.org/the-aztecs-facts-information-for-kids-2/

Fun Educational YouTube Videos for Kids about the Aztecs:

- The Aztecs: All You Need to Know
  https://www.youtube.com/watch?v=urFpctOmJZY
- The Aztecs for Kids
  https://www.youtube.com/watch?v=nWxqnZeELbU
- 10 Amazing Facts About the Aztecs for Kids
  https://www.youtube.com/watch?v=kAL-o4sR6As

Image Sources

[1] Jay Galvin, CC BY-SA 2.0 (https://creativecommons.org/licenses/by/2.0/deed.en), via Wikimedia Commons; https://commons.wikimedia.org/wiki/File:Huapalcalco_(Pyramid)_Archaeological_Site.jpg

[2] Maribel Ponce Ixba (frida27ponce), CC BY 2.0 <https://creativecommons.org/licenses/by/2.0>, via Wikimedia Commons; https://commons.wikimedia.org/wiki/File:San_Lorenzo_Monument_3.jpg

[3] Arien Zwegers, CC BY-SA 2.0 (https://creativecommons.org/licenses/by/2.0/deed.en), via Wikimedia Commons; https://commons.wikimedia.org/wiki/File:Tula,_Pyramid_B_(20660295926).jpg

[4] Ricardo David Sanchez, CC BY-SA 3.0 (https://creativecommons.org/licenses/by-sa/3.0/deed.en), via Wikimedia Commons; https://commons.wikimedia.org/wiki/File:Teotihuacán-5973.JPG

[5] Sémhur, CC BY-SA 4.0 (https//creativecommons.org/licenses/by-sa/4.0/), via Wikimedia Commons. https://commons.wikimedia.org/wiki/File:Basin_of_Mexico_1519_map-en.svg

[6] Anaporti, CC BY-SA 3.0 (https://creativecommons.org/licenses/by-sa/3.0/deed.en), via Wikimedia Commons; https://commons.wikimedia.org/wiki/File:Teopanzolco_Ana_2.jpg

[7] Chmouel Boudinah, CC BY-SA 3.0 (https://creativecommons.org/licenses/by-sa/3.0/deed.en), via Wikimedia Commons; https://commons.wikimedia.org/wiki/File:Statue_of_Foundation_of_Tenochtitlan.jpg

[8] Gary Todd from Xinzheng, China, CC0, via Wikimedia Commons; https://commons.wikimedia.org/wiki/File:Painting_of_Tenochtitlan-Tlatelolco_on_Lake_Texcoco_(9755215791).jpg

[9] Joe Ravi, CC BY-SA 3.0 (https://creativecommons.org/licenses/by-sa/3.0/deed.en), via Wikimedia Commons; https://commons.wikimedia.org/wiki/File:Tlatelolco_Marketplace.JPG

[10] https://commons.wikimedia.org/wiki/File:Codex_Mendoza_folio_67r_bottom.jpg

[11] Badseed based on work by historicair which in turn was based on Madman2001's work. CC BY-SA 3.0; https://commons.wikimedia.org/w/index.php?curid=1706112

[12] https://commons.wikimedia.org/wiki/File:Codex_Zouche-Nuttall_(folio_89).JPG

[13] Sailko, CC BY-SA 3.0 (https://creativecommons.org/licenses/by/3.0/deed.en), via Wikimedia Commons; https://commons.wikimedia.org/wiki/File:Mesoamerica,_puebla,_cholula,_mixteca-puebla_(nahua-mixteca),_ciotola_con_piede,_1200-1521_ca._02.jpg

[14] INAH, Canon, CC BY-SA 4.0 <https://creativecommons.org/licenses/by-sa/4.0>, via Wikimedia Commons; https://commons.wikimedia.org/wiki/File:Piedra_del_Sol.png

[15] https://commons.wikimedia.org/wiki/File:Codex_Mendoza_folio_47r.jpg

[16] https://commons.wikimedia.org/wiki/File:Moctezuma_I,_the_Fifth_Aztec_King.png

[17] TlatelolcoTV, CC BY-SA 3.0 <https://creativecommons.org/licenses/by-sa/3.0>, via Wikimedia Commons https://commons.wikimedia.org/wiki/File:Zona_Arqueológica_de_Tlatelolco,_TlatelolcoTV_23.jpg

[18] https://commons.wikimedia.org/wiki/File:Huitzilopochtli_telleriano.jpg

[19] https://commons.wikimedia.org/wiki/File:Tezcatlipoca.png

[20] https://commons.wikimedia.org/wiki/File:Quetzalcoatl_V.png

[21] https://commons.wikimedia.org/wiki/File:Tonalpohualli_Aztec_calendar.jpg

[22] http://commons.wikimedia.org/wiki/File:Aztec_shared_meal.jpg

[23] https://commons.wikimedia.org/wiki/File:Aztec_drums,_Florentine_Codex..jpg

[24] https://commons.wikimedia.org/wiki/File:The_Aztec_Ritual_Offering_Against_Drought_WDL6750.png
[25] https://commons.wikimedia.org/wiki/File:Moctezuma_Mendoza.jpg
[26] https://commons.wikimedia.org/wiki/File:Battle_Spanish_Otomies_Metztitlan.jpg
[27] User:JEDIKNIGHT1970, CC BY-SA 3.0 <http://creativecommons.org/licenses/by-sa/3.0/>, via Wikimedia Commons; https://commons.wikimedia.org/wiki/File:Cuauhtemoc_cropped.jpg
[28] https://commons.wikimedia.org/wiki/File:Hernan_Fernando_Cortes.jpg
[29] GAED, CC BY-SA 3.0 <https://creativecommons.org/licenses/by-sa/3.0>, via Wikimedia Commons; https://commons.wikimedia.org/wiki/File:Metro_Moctezuma_01.jpg
[30] Jesús Gorriti, CC BY-SA 2.0 (https://creativecommons.org/licenses/by-sa/2.0/deed.en, via Wikimedia Commons; https://commons.wikimedia.org/wiki/File:Partial_view_Templo_Mayor.jpg
[31] https://commons.wikimedia.org/wiki/File:Coat_of_arms_of_Mexico.svg

www.ingramcontent.com/pod-product-compliance
Lightning Source LLC
Chambersburg PA
CBHW070321010526
44107CB00004B/379